Module 8: Presentations

Introduction

This module will familiarise you with the steps involved in preparing and delivering an oral presentation. Being able to give an effective oral presentation is an essential skill in both academic and professional life, and prospective employers often look for experience and proficiency in speaking to large groups.

In higher or further education you may be asked to give presentations (alone or in groups) for a variety of reasons: you might be given a topic to speak on by your tutor, you might be required to give a summary of your essay research, or you might be asked to inform a class of your laboratory research methods and results. Such talks may be formally assessed as coursework or may function as a more informal information-sharing experience. By following the tasks in this module, you will learn how to optimise your communication skills in this area and develop confidence through a series of micro-tasks.

Contents

1 About presentations

At the end of this unit, you will:

- recognise what makes a good presentation
- understand the process of preparing a presentation

Task 1 What makes a good presentation?

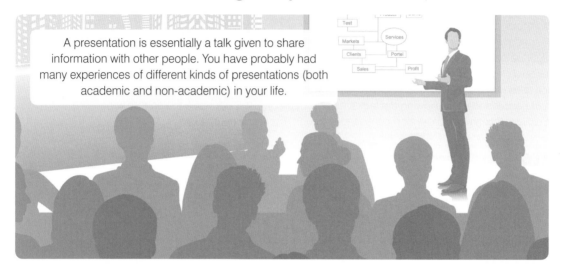

A presentation is essentially a talk given to share information with other people. You have probably had many experiences of different kinds of presentations (both academic and non-academic) in your life.

1.1 Think about the presentations you have seen in the past.

Consider as many different aspects of a presentation as possible (for example, the speaker, the topic, the material, the language) and work in small groups to discuss the questions.

a. What makes a good presentation?

b. What makes a bad presentation?

1.2 Presentations benefit from good preparation. The rest of this unit will focus on the steps involved in planning to deliver a successful presentation and on the importance of knowing how you will be evaluated.

Work with a partner and take it in turns to deliver mini-talks on these questions. You should speak for 1–2 minutes only. When you listen to your partner, make notes on the main points.

Student A: What are the essential steps needed to thoroughly prepare for a presentation? Give some explanation for each one.

Student B: What are the main criteria that can be used to assess an oral presentation? Give some explanation for each one.

1.3 Discuss how you felt about delivering these mini-talks. What aspects of presentation-giving would you like to improve?

Task 2 Planning checklist

2.1 Compare the points raised during the talks in Task 1.2 with the following checklist. Tick the tasks that were mentioned.

Planning checklist

☐ Choose your topic

In some cases, the topic will be given to you by your tutor. If not, check that it is appropriate with your tutor before the next step.

☐ Check that you know exactly what is expected of you

If your presentation will be assessed, make sure you understand the grading criteria. You should also be clear on how much time you will have.

☐ Identify your audience

Think about who your audience will be. For example, are you presenting to students who know something about your topic or to people from outside your academic field?

☐ Conduct research

Research will help you know enough about your topic for the presentation. Think about where you can find the information you need (the library, the Internet). References to the sources you have used should be included in a bibliography.

☐ Decide on your focus

It is important to know the purpose of your presentation: What are you trying to show or prove to your audience? This will help you focus the topic to a manageable number of main points within the time available.

☐ Plan what you are going to say

Write notes to help you remember the main points of your talk. You should not, however, just read from a script.

☐ Choose and prepare visual aids

Which visual aids will help you communicate your message best?

☐ Rehearse your presentation

Practise delivering your finished presentation. You should do this as many times as possible, speaking out loud and using your visual aids.

Task 3 Grading criteria

If your presentation is going to be assessed, you should find out in advance what assessment criteria will be used. This will help you to plan and give a more effective presentation.

3.1 Make a list of the major criteria that can be used to assess a presentation. Use ideas from the talks in Task 1.2 and add new points. For each item, explain what it may include.

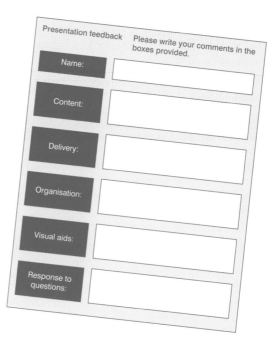

Organisation: The presentation is well planned and has a clear and logical structure.

Reflect

Find an example of an academic presentation online. Your tutor can help you look or you can search on YouTube or TED Talks, for example.

As you watch:

- Make notes on its strengths and weaknesses, using the presentation grading criteria from Task 3.
- Make a list of any improvements you can suggest.

Group presentations

At the end of this unit, you will:

- understand how to organise the preparation process
- understand how to share roles and responsibilities

You will sometimes be expected to give a presentation as a member of a group. In this unit you will explore the dynamics of group presentations and then work with some other students to prepare a presentation on an academic topic. Your tutor will help you decide on this topic. Then, for the rest of this module, you will use the tasks in each unit to help you plan and present your talk together. If you would like more information on teamwork, you can refer to the *Group Work & Projects* TASK module.

Task 1 Advantages and disadvantages

1.1 **Discuss the following questions in small groups and make notes.**

a. What are the advantages of giving a group presentation?

b. What are the disadvantages of giving a group presentation?

Task 2 Working together

A group presentation involves team effort. It is always clear when students do not work with their group, as their pieces of the presentation do not fit together with the other group members' pieces on the day of delivery.

2.1 **Work in your presentation group. Look back at the *Planning checklist* in Task 2.1 and discuss which of the tasks you should work on as a team, and which ones could be done individually. Write your answers in the table. (You may also decide that some tasks should be tackled individually first and then discussed in a group.)**

team tasks	individual tasks

2.2 **Would the following activities be team tasks or individual tasks? Add them to the table.**

a. set deadlines

b. select a team co-ordinator

c. conduct research on the presentation topic

d. plan who will do or say what

2

Task 3 Group planning

How will you organise your talk as a group? You will have to share the work equally and you will need to meet and plan with the other members outside of class time in order to prepare a successful presentation. It is important to keep a record of the planning for your presentation. These records will aid your organisation. If your group presentation is going to be assessed, these records may also contribute towards the marks that you are awarded.

3.1 **Work with your presentation group to read the activities in the box. Choose the ones that you think will be most useful for your group and put them in a logical order.**

Presentation planning

- Share responsibilities equally

- Set up a way to share documents (Dropbox, Google Docs, etc.)

- Distribute meeting notes to other members

- Discuss what the presentation assignment means

- Divide the presentation assignment into smaller tasks

- Record the names and contact information for all group members

- Write meeting notes with action points

- Set deadlines for the completion of tasks

- Give each other feedback

- Arrange a preliminary meeting to agree how to proceed

- Schedule regular meetings in advance

Presentation planning

_____

_____

_____

_____

_____

_____

_____

_____

_____

_____

_____

Task 4 Group work

Practise working with your group members to prepare and deliver mini-presentations. At the end, you will give each other feedback in order to help each other improve. Take it in turns to present and to give feedback.

4.1 With a partner (from your group), choose one of the following topics. You have five minutes to prepare a two-minute presentation. Make some notes to help you during your talk.

> The world is better off than it was 60 years ago

> Animals should not be kept in zoos

> The sale of cigarettes should be made illegal

> Everyone should study at least one foreign language

> Group work can benefit everyone involved

> School students should be required to wear a uniform

4.2 Using your notes, deliver the talk to the remaining member(s) of your group. They will listen and then give you feedback. You can use the grading criteria from Unit 1, Task 3, if you wish.

Reflect

Think about how every member of your group can take responsibility for the preparation of your presentation.

Record who is responsible for each task in the table. This will ensure that the work is shared equally and that nothing is forgotten.

name	responsibility	action

Plan what you will do if one of the group members does not complete his/her responsibilities. How will the other members of the group deal with this sort of problem?

3 Content

At the end of this unit, you will:

- understand how to define your topic and purpose
- be able to plan your presentation
- be aware of appropriate presentation structure

Task 1 Defining your purpose

Each group should have agreed on a topic. At this stage it is helpful to clearly define the purpose of your presentation, as this will help you decide the direction you will go in as you explore the topic further. You will then be able to develop your presentation outline.

1.1 **Individually, think about the topic and the main purpose of your presentation. Does it fit into one or more of these categories?**

- ☐ Persuasive
- ☐ Evaluative
- ☐ Informative
- ☐ Problem–solution
- ☐ Compare–contrast
- ☐ Other

1.2 **Compare your answers with the other members of your group.**

1.3 **Discuss which information from your research can best support your purpose.**

Once your group has agreed on the topic and purpose of the presentation, you can start planning.

Task 2 Presentation structure

It is now time to plan what you are going to say by preparing the content in a clear and logical way. This will enable your audience to both engage with your presentation and recall what you have said.

2.1 **Study the diagram and be ready to explain the structure of a presentation to the rest of the class.**

2.2 **In your presentation groups, give a brief overview of the following to the rest of the class:**

- the topic of your presentation
- the main points of your presentation

Task 3 Planning your presentation

3.1 Continue in your presentation group and plan your introduction. Answer these three questions together to create an introduction that you feel will get the attention of your audience.

Make sure that one of the members in your group keeps a clear record of the points you make.

- What will your first sentence be?
- How will you introduce yourself and your group?
- How will you introduce your topic and explain why it is important?

3.2 Continue in your presentation group. Think about the main points that you would like to make; these should all be related to your topic. For each main point, give some support: this could be detail, explanation or evidence, and will come from your research. If contrasting opinions exist, make sure you consider both sides of the argument.

Make sure that one member of the group keeps a record under the following headings:

First main point:
    Support:
Second main point:
    Support:
Third main point:
    Support:
Fourth main point:
    Support:

The conclusion should clearly summarise what your presentation has shown.

As your conclusion is the final thing your audience will hear, it is particularly important that it should make an impact. For example, when you go over points you have already made in the main body, make sure you do this clearly and concisely without simply repeating what you have said before. It can be useful to identify the key points you want the audience to remember after the presentation; these are also known as 'take-home' points.

3.3 Work on your conclusions in your presentation group, then present your conclusions to the class. Ask your classmates to identify the key points. Did they note all of the points you wanted them to remember?

After the conclusion, you will need to bring your presentation to an end.

Additional steps that you can add at the end of your presentation include:

- Providing a bibliography (as a handout or as a final slide on-screen)
- Inviting questions from the audience
- Saying a final thank you to the audience

3.4 In your group, discuss how you will end your presentation. Also discuss whether you want to provide handouts to your audience and, if so, what these handouts will include. Will you distribute them at the beginning or the end of the presentation? How will you handle audience questions?

3

Task 4 Preparing notes

Giving a presentation is not the same as reading an essay out loud. This is why it is useful to write your presentation in note form rather than continuous prose. You should already know what you want to say; the notes just provide a framework so you can keep to the structure you have planned.

4.1 Discuss in groups the presentation you did in Unit 1. Did you use notes to help you present? Discuss together the advantages and disadvantages of the following methods:

Memorising your talk

Writing a list of bullet points on sheets of paper

Writing each key idea on a separate notecard

Using the notes function within your presentation software

Using the screen as a prompt (without additional notes)

4.2 In your presentation groups, use the information from Task 3 to write your own set of notes. Take account of anything you have learnt from the discussion in Task 4.1.

Reflect

For some conferences you will be asked to provide an abstract for your presentation.

Review the outline plan you made for your presentation and use it to write a 100-word abstract of your talk. It should reflect the purpose of your presentation and highlight your main points. Compare your abstract with those written by your group members.

4 Visual aids

At the end of this unit, you will:
- be more familiar with a range of appropriate visual aids
- be able to design and use visual aids effectively

Task 1 Why use visual aids?

Visual aids can greatly enhance an oral presentation by highlighting key points or information. Presentation software can help you structure your talk clearly. Diagrams and images can convey ideas quickly, can engage the audience, and can help them understand information.

1.1 What information in your presentation will benefit most from visual support?

Task 2 Choosing and using visual aids

There are many kinds of visual aids available. Think about presentations and lectures you have attended in the past and consider the visual aids that were used.

2.1 Discuss with a partner which of the following you have either seen or used. What do you think are the advantages and disadvantages of each of them for the audience and/or for the speaker?

visual aid	advantages	disadvantages
posters		
presentation software (Microsoft PowerPoint, Prezi)		
videos		
whiteboard		
printed handouts		
props		

2.2 Visual aids are useful to help get your message across to your audience. Nevertheless, even with good visual aids, things can go wrong if they are not used appropriately.

Look at the list of *don'ts* and discuss why each point is a problem.

DON'T:

- crowd too much information into one visual
- stand in front of the visual aid
- read directly from the main screen or visual
- put unimportant details in the visual
- forget to talk about information in a visual
- use a font that is too small
- put visuals in a different order to that of information in the presentation

2.3 Work in groups to discuss the following slide. What problems can you identify?

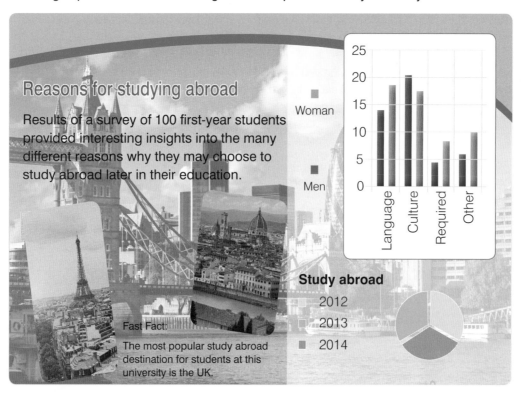

Task 3 Choosing what to write and what to say

Once you have chosen a visual aid for your presentation, it is important to prepare carefully.
You need to carefully balance the written words and images on your visual aid with what you say.

3.1 With a partner, discuss the problems of:

- writing too much text, without providing any visuals
- showing an image without any explanation

3.2 Work in small groups. The slide below suffers from 'text overload' (too many unnecessary words on one slide). Reduce and simplify the text. Consider what words will remain on the slide and what information you can communicate verbally.

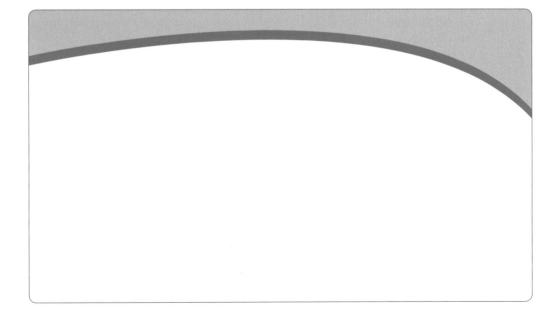

Why should university students study a foreign language?

**Learning a foreign language can benefit you in a number of important ways.
The top reasons include:**

- Learning another language can help you gain increased intercultural awareness. You can become what is known as a 'global citizen'.
- Statistics prove that being able to speak another language can greatly improve your employability. Nowadays many employers are looking for job applicants who can speak one or more foreign languages.
- Languages may offer you increased mobility and may open up exciting opportunities for travel all around the world.
- You will experience personal satisfaction as you acquire new skills.

Task 4 Preparing posters

Poster presentations are a popular type of visual aid and it is quite likely that you will present or view posters while you are a student.

4.1 What are the key differences between posters and presentation software such as PowerPoint?

4.2 Preparing a poster may seem different to preparing a PowerPoint presentation, but the principles are essentially the same. The following example indicates the questions you should ask yourself in order to prepare any visual aid. If you can answer each question with confidence, then you know what you have to do.

question	answer
a. What visual aid am I going to use?	Poster presentation.
b. What is it?	A poster is a large document (usually mounted on a card backing) that can be used to communicate your research at a presentation or meeting. A poster usually contains both text and pictures/graphs. The presenter generally stands next to his/her poster and explains information where necessary.
c. Are there any special requirements or constraints?	Make sure you know the size of the poster you are expected to produce, as this is usually set in advance.
d. What materials/ equipment do I need?	You will need the appropriate software and design templates. If you do not have access to a specialised printer, you will have to print out individual sections on A4 paper and put them together.
e. How will the content be organised?	A poster presentation is one large document that is generally subdivided into some or all of the following sections: • Title • Introduction • Methods • Results • Discussion • Conclusion • References
f. What is the best layout?	A poster has to be legible from a distance, so the most important advice here is to have limited text and interesting graphics. Techniques are: • use short sentences and bullets • use large font size • use pictures, charts and graphs to illustrate information • use colour carefully to add interest
g. How do I put it all together?	Here is one possible layout: <table><tr><td colspan="3">Title</td></tr><tr><td>Introduction</td><td>Graphs/Pictures</td><td>Conclusion</td></tr></table>

4.3 Work with a partner to choose another type of visual aid from the table in Task 2.1. Apply the same seven questions to the visual aid and complete the table below.

question	answer
a. What visual aid am I going to use?	
b. What is it?	
c. Are there any special requirements or constraints?	
d. What materials/ equipment do I need?	
e. How will the content be organised?	
f. What is the best layout?	
g. How do I put it all together?	

Reflect

You need to plan carefully to use your visual aids most effectively and manage unexpected problems. Answer the questions.

a.   Where will you stand in relation to the screen or your poster?

b.   Are there any visuals or graphics that you will want to point out or interact with?

c.   What sort of back-up plan do you have for your presentation in case of technical problems?

d.   Do you know the set-up of the space where you will deliver your presentation?

Delivery

At the end of this unit, you will:

- be more familiar with the language of presentations
- be able to use appropriate body language

Once you have researched and prepared the content of a talk, it is essential to focus on its delivery.

Task 1 The language of presentations

The language you use can help indicate the structure of your presentation and guide the audience.

1.1 Match the functions (a–e) with the appropriate groups of phrases (1–5). These phrases are known as 'signposts' because they help to clarify where your presentation is going.

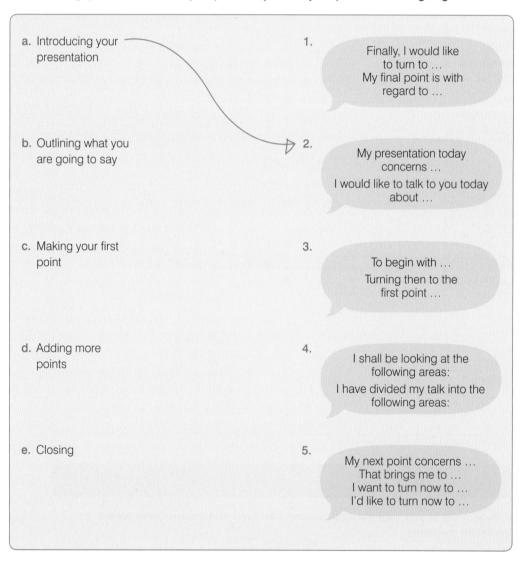

a. Introducing your presentation

b. Outlining what you are going to say

c. Making your first point

d. Adding more points

e. Closing

1.
> Finally, I would like to turn to …
> My final point is with regard to …

2.
> My presentation today concerns …
> I would like to talk to you today about …

3.
> To begin with …
> Turning then to the first point …

4.
> I shall be looking at the following areas:
> I have divided my talk into the following areas:

5.
> My next point concerns …
> That brings me to …
> I want to turn now to …
> I'd like to turn now to …

1.2 Similar phrases can be used to signal when you are doing other things within each stage of your presentation. Match the functions (f–j) to the phrases (6–10).

f. Giving emphasis (for example, in your conclusion)

6.
It must be remembered that …
It should be emphasised that …
I would like to underline the point that …

g. Adding more information

7.
To illustrate this point, …
For instance, …
A good example of this is …

h. Making a generalisation

8.
In addition, …
Furthermore, …
Not only … but also …
I should add that …

i. Balancing an argument, stating opposing views

9.
On the whole, …
Generally speaking, …

j. Giving an example

10.
On the one hand …
but on the other hand …

Task 2 Using your voice effectively

Using your voice effectively can enhance the interest and intelligibility of your presentation. No matter how good your research, content and visual aids are, a monotonous and unenthusiastic delivery will detract from the overall impression you make.

2.1 Work in small groups. One student should read the introduction to this book aloud as quickly as possible without looking up. The rest of the group will listen with books closed. When the speaker has finished, you should all discuss the effect that listening to a talk like that had on the listeners.

2.2 Discuss how you can use each of the following features to add enthusiasm and interest to your speech.

Volume

Be sure to speak loudly enough so that everyone in the room can hear you. Keep looking up so that your voice carries clearly.

Speed

_____

_____

Intonation

_____

_____

Pauses

_____

_____

Emphasis

_____

_____

Task 3 Body language

In addition to your command of English, your body language will also affect how your presentation is received.

3.1 Read the list of some of the things that speakers often do during a presentation. Work with a partner to discuss what impression each one may give the audience. Can you add anything to the list?

smile at the audience

sit down

walk around

look only at notes

use hand gestures

make eye contact with the audience

play with hair/change in pocket/earring, etc.

lean against a wall

point at the audience

3.2 Body language is not universal. If your body language and gestures are misinterpreted, it can result in confusion. Discuss the questions in groups of three to five.

    a.   What sort of differences have you noticed in the way that people from other cultures use gestures and body language?

    b.   Have you ever experienced a communication breakdown due to a misunderstanding about the meaning of a gesture?

5

Task 4 Rehearsing your presentation

It is essential to rehearse your presentation thoroughly before the day of your presentation. This will help you identify any problems with language, organisation, visuals, group dynamics or timing. If you do encounter any issues, you will still have time to make changes or improvements. Being well-prepared can also help reduce nerves.

4.1 In your presentation group, answer the questions.

a. Where and when are you going to rehearse the finished presentation together?

_____

b. Who will watch and give feedback on the rehearsal?

_____

c. Are you going to record or video yourselves? How?

_____

d. How will you time it?

_____

e. When will your group review the rehearsal and discuss final changes?

_____

Reflect

How can you improve your presentation delivery?

Record yourself or stand in front of a mirror as you rehearse your presentation. Refer back to some of the ideas in this unit and think about changes in your language and body language that you feel will be useful for you in formal speaking situations in the future.

Web work

Website 1

Presentation planner

http://www2.elc.polyu.edu.hk/cill/tools/presplan.htm

Review

This website is designed to help you plan, organise and write your presentation by following a series of prompts. It will also provide notecards and a script of your finished product, and a record of what your presentation will sound like.

Task

Once you have a finished presentation, use this presentation planner to do a test run of your talk. If you are pleased with the finished result, take advantage of the option to print out notecards.

Website 2

Using PowerPoint in the classroom

http://www.actden.com/pp/

Review

The tutorial takes you through all the steps in creating and editing PowerPoint slides.

Task

If you still feel that you need more help with PowerPoint, try the tutorial offered here.

Extension activities

Activity 1

Practise your PowerPoint skills by making slides to illustrate the key steps of the Planning checklist in Unit 1.

Look back at the *Planning checklist* in Unit 1 and make PowerPoint slides to give a short presentation of this information. What information would you include on the slide, and what would you say to illustrate the main point?

Compare your work with another student. Have you handled the checklist in similar ways?

Activity 2

Some presentations require you to conduct your own research and then present the results to your class. In this activity, you will give a presentation detailing the results of a short questionnaire on student attitudes to a particular aspect of university life, e.g., exams, seminars, oral presentations, note-taking.

There are several parts to the activity:

a. **Design a short questionnaire to find out information about students' attitudes to the aspect of university life that you have chosen.**

   You could include questions on:

   - Extent of experience with …
   - Views on advantages and disadvantages of …
   - Self-rating of skill at …
   - Opinion of usefulness of … skills beyond university

b. **Obtain responses from at least 10 other students.**

c. **Compile your results and share them with the rest of your class in a presentation with visual aids.**

Glossary

balance an argument (v) To make sure that both sides of an argument have been considered and explained.

bibliography (n) A list of references to sources cited in the text of a piece of academic writing or a book. It should consist of an alphabetical list of books, papers, journal articles and websites, and is usually found at the end of the work. It may also include texts suggested by the author for further reading.

body language (n) Non-verbal communication of feelings and ideas through movements of the body. For example, certain body movements such as fidgeting and yawning may indicate boredom.

checklist (n) A list of tasks to do or aspects to consider when planning and preparing for an event such as an academic assignment, journey or party.

communication breakdown (n) A situation in which individuals or groups are unable to understand each other at all due to differences in language, culture or belief.

constraint (n) Something that places a limit or restriction on what you want to do. For example, if you are doing a presentation, there may be time constraints.

co-ordinator (n) Someone who is responsible for arranging how a group or workforce shares out duties and for ensuring that the final product or results are brought together effectively.

deadline (n) The date or time by which something needs to be completed. In academic situations, deadlines are normally given for handing in essays and assignments.

delivery (n) The way in which someone speaks in public. For example, when giving a presentation, the delivery refers to the language and style used, the ability to connect with the audience and how effectively the message is conveyed.

dynamics (n) The way that things work together to produce energy and results. For example, it is important that group dynamics are effective so that everyone works well together.

emphasise (v) To highlight or draw attention to something that is important.

evidence (n) Information and data that establish whether something is true or not.

framework (n) A basic structure that is an outline of something more detailed.

gesture (n) (v) 1 (n) An action meant to communicate an idea non-verbally or to emphasise a thought or meaning. 2 (v) To make such an action. For example, putting one's hand over one's heart indicates sincerity.

grading criteria (n) The basis on which something will be assessed. It is important to know what the grading criteria consist of when writing an academic assignment. For example, a piece of work may be assessed on grammatical accuracy and/or how well it is presented, or it may be evaluated on its content alone.

handout (n) Paper-based information that is given out by the lecturer or speaker in a lecture, seminar or tutorial. It usually gives a summary, bibliography or extra information connected with the lecture topic. It may also be a worksheet.

layout (n) The way that things are positioned within a space. For example, the way text, pictures and diagrams are arranged on a page or computer screen.

outline (n) (v) 1 (n) A rough, often point-form, sketch of the main ideas in a text or presentation. 2 (v) To give or make a rough sketch of the main ideas or events in a text or presentation.

poster presentation (n) A presentation that involves displaying posters with information and pictures or diagrams. The audience generally reads the posters while the presenter stands next to them and explains information where necessary.

PowerPoint (n) The (Microsoft) brand name for a type of software known as a presentation program. The software enables users to write and design slideshows for presentations. The slides may be viewed on a computer, projected onto a screen and/or printed out.

presentation (n) A short lecture, talk or demonstration (usually formal) given in front of an audience. The speaker prepares and structures his/her presentation in advance and will often use visual aids or realia to illustrate it.

reference (n) (v) 1 (n) Acknowledgment of the sources of ideas and information that you use in written work and oral presentations. 2 (v) To acknowledge or mention sources of information.

rehearse (v) To practise a speech, dialogue, play or presentation that is going to be performed in front of an audience.

role (n) The part someone plays in a group (or any situation that involves interacting with other people). In some situations, these roles may be flexible or unspoken; in others they are well-defined, such as the leader of a team.

signposts (n) Words, phrases or other organisational features such as headings and opening sentences in a text that help the audience or reader identify a section. For example, a lecturer may signpost the conclusion of a talk by prefacing it with 'To sum up …'.

source (n) Something (usually a book, article or other text) that supplies you with information. In an academic context, sources used in essays and reports must be acknowledged.

structure (n) (v) 1 (n) A framework or arrangement of several parts, put together in a particular way.
2 (v) In academic terms, to put together ideas or arguments in a logical way for an essay or presentation.

support (n) (v) 1 (n) Evidence and ideas that back up an argument.
2 (v) To back up an argument with evidence.

visual aid (n) An object or image that is used in a lecture, presentation or lesson to help clarify information visually. For example, diagrams, pictures, posters, models and video are commonly used visual aids.

Notes

Notes

Notes

Notes

Notes

Notes

Notes

Published by
Garnet Publishing Ltd
8 Southern Court
South Street
Reading RG1 4QS, UK

ISBN 978 1 78260 183 8

British Library Cataloguing-in-Publication Data
A catalogue record for this book is available from the British Library.

Production
Project Manager: Clare Chandler
Editorial team: Clare Chandler, Sophia Hopton,
                              Martin Moore
Design & Layout: Madeleine Maddock
Photography: iStockphoto, Shutterstock

Garnet Publishing and the authors of TASK would like to thank the staff and students of the International Foundation Programme at the University of Reading for their respective roles in the development of these teaching materials.

Garnet Publishing would like to thank Jane Brooks for her contribution to the First edition of the TASK series.

All website URLs provided in this publication were correct at the time of printing. If any URL does not work, please contact your tutor, who will help you find similar resources.

Printed and bound in Lebanon by International Press:
interpress@int-press.com

Acknowledgements
Page 11: Task 2.1, use of Prezi presentation program name, used with permission from Prezi Inc.

Pages 11, 14, 21, 22 and 23:
           use of PowerPoint® presentation program name, used with permission from Microsoft.

Transferable
Academic
Skills
Kit

TASK

Presentations

University Foundation Study

The **Transferable Academic Skills Kit (TASK)** is a flexible learning resource that has been carefully designed to develop the key transferable skills that promote students' success in university and college study. Whether you are a student or a teacher, the TASK series provides a tried and tested teaching and learning tool suitable for a broad range of academic disciplines.

A series of supported exercises relates theory to practice and provides students with the tools to develop a framework of skills that can then be used in a wide range of contexts, both inside and outside the academic world. Each module also has web work and extension activities that offer additional information and practice relating to the skills covered in that module.

TASK can be followed as a complete course or individual modules can be selected to address specific needs, building the skills required by home and international students at all levels.

The series has been created by members of the International Foundation Programme, provided by the International Study and Language Institute (ISLI) at the University of Reading.

The complete TASK series comprises:
1 Academic Culture
2 Group Work & Projects
3 Critical Thinking
4 Essay Writing
5 Scientific Writing
6 Research & Online Sources
7 Referencing & Avoiding Plagiarism
8 Presentations
9 Assessments, Exams & Revision
10 Numeracy

The International Study and Language Institute (ISLI) at the University of Reading has 40 years' experience in providing academic training to international students. It has a long-standing, worldwide reputation for the quality of its tuition, materials development and the support given to students during their time in higher education.

ISBN 978-1-78260-183-8

www.garneteducation.com

2

Transferable
Academic
Skills
Kit

TASK

University Foundation Study

Group Work & Projects

Student's Book

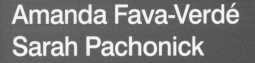

Amanda Fava-Verdé
Sarah Pachonick

Anthony Manning

Clare Nukui

Andrew O'Cain

Elisabeth Wilding

University of
READING | *Garnet*
EDUCATION